Nobody Knows But Me

FASTBACK® Romance

Nobody Knows But Me

EVE BUNTING

GLOBE FEARON
Pearson Learning Group

FASTBACK® ROMANCE BOOKS

Fifteen
For Always
The Girl in the Painting
Just Like Everyone Else
Maggie

Nobody Knows But Me
A Part of the Dream
Survival Camp
Tomorrow!
Two Different Girls

Cover *border* Jules Frazier/Getty Images, Inc. All photography © Pearson Education, Inc. (PEI) unless specifically noted.

Copyright © 2004 by Pearson Education, Inc., publishing as Globe Fearon®, an imprint of Pearson Learning Group, 299 Jefferson Road, Parsippany, NJ 07054. All rights reserved. No part of this book may be reproduced or transmitted in any form or by any means, electronic or mechanical, including photocopying, recording, or by any information storage and retrieval system, without permission in writing from the publisher. For information regarding permission(s), write to Rights and Permissions Department.

Globe Fearon® and Fastback® are registered trademarks of Globe Fearon, Inc.

ISBN 0-13-024568-2
Printed in the United States of America
1 2 3 4 5 6 7 8 9 10   07 06 05 04 03

1-800-321-3106
www.pearsonlearning.com

George stopped the car in front of Ellen's house. His arm slid along the seat behind her shoulders, and she knew he was going to kiss her. Their first kiss.

The light from the streetlamp shone in his dark eyes and turned his black hair almost blue. Ellen felt her heart begin to beat faster, faster. She closed her eyes.

And it was then that the terrible thing happened. Her mind did a switch, and suddenly it was Leo Carlton kissing her, not George. Those were Leo's hands on her shoulders. That was Leo's cheek, a little rough against hers.

She pulled away and opened her eyes. Not Leo. George. George!

"I like you a lot, Ellen," George said.

"I like you too," Ellen stammered.

"So, it's all set then. Tomorrow night we'll split up after the game so we can change out of our crummy band uniforms," George said. "Then I'll pick you up here. And we'll go straight to the football dance. Right?"

"Right," Ellen said. "I'm really looking forward to going." And don't probe into why you're looking forward to it, she warned herself silently. She pushed the ghost of Leo Carlton away angrily and smiled at George.

He walked her to her door. And this time his good-night kiss blotted out any thoughts she had of Leo.

"See you," George said.

"See you." Ellen hugged her arms tightly

about her and closed her eyes. George was nice, really, really nice.

But that night, lying sleepless in bed, the dreams of Leo came as they always did.

He'd be at the football dance. All the varsity team would be there. He'd come striding in, bigger, taller, more terrific than anyone in the room. His mane of golden hair! And his eyes, they were golden too. Leo the Lion, king of the jungle. But she wasn't going with George just so she could see Leo, just so she could be in the same room with him. She wasn't!

Ellen punched her pillow and turned it over. George! George had come to Muir High only two months ago. He'd joined the band right away, and then she'd noticed him in algebra class. George was smart. He wasn't sticking his hand up all the time and shouting out answers, but if Mr. Andrews did ask him something, he always knew.

Sometimes old Andrews even asked George to figure something out for him. Leo Carlton was in algebra too.

Ellen sat up, punched her pillow again, and lay down.

She sat right behind Leo. Of course, he didn't know she was there and didn't care either. He was too busy watching Vicki Smith. And Ellen watched him watching Vicki. It was like some kind of crazy merry-go-round. Hey, she thought, what if George is watching me, watching him, watching her? That's funny. No, it isn't funny at all.

The living room clock struck 1 a.m.

Ellen got out of bed and took her flute from its case on the dresser. Many nights she'd done this, playing softly to herself so that the sound wouldn't carry upstairs and wake her parents. She sat on the corner of the crumpled blanket.

*Nobody knows how I feel about you,
Nobody knows but me.
Nobody knows how the touch of your hand
Changes my world to a new wonderland.
Nobody knows but me.*

It was one of the Muir band tunes, a lilting, swinging melody that they played at the halftime shows. The melody conjured up for Ellen the football stadium, the stands crammed with people, the dry, brown turf. But the words, the words belonged to Leo.

Oh, Leo, she thought. Why isn't it you who likes me a lot? Why isn't it you taking me to the dance?

She gently put her flute back in its case and climbed into bed again. As usual the music had comforted her. The sadness was gentler now. And tomorrow, tomorrow she'd keep Leo out of her mind. Of course, the band would be playing at the game, and she'd be sitting there, watching, hearing Leo's name over the loudspeaker. Well, try anyway, Ellen. Just try.

She was trying. Sitting in the front row of the band seats at the game, she was trying.

"Ladies and gentlemen, the Muir Monarchs," the loudspeaker boomed, and the band exploded into the Monarch fight song.

Ellen forced herself not to look for number 60 as the red and gold swarm rushed onto the field. But it was hard to miss him when he was the first one out, leading the pack. The first one to break through the paper barrier that Vicki and the other song girls held.

Number 60 stood to attention for the national anthem.

He cradled his helmet, and the wind blew his hair into a golden halo. The flute suddenly felt slippery in Ellen's hands, and she didn't think she had enough breath left for the last star-spangled notes. How did a person get to be this way about another person? It was as mysterious and unpredictable as a summer cold.

On the sidelines the song girls and cheerleaders turned cartwheels and did a kicky little dance.

"Would you look at those goony girls!" Tammy Townsend said. Tammy played flute next to Ellen. "Honestly! I think this year's group is worse than last year's."

Ellen glanced sideways at her. There was a sound in Tammy's voice that Ellen had heard before. And she remembered when. The band had been waiting for a football practice to end. The players had been running some kind of formation on the field.

"Get a load of those dumb jocks," one of the drummers had sneered. "Not a brain in the bunch."

George had spoken quickly. "Why don't you just shut up, Lewis. Have you ever taken a look at a game playbook? Man, football is more complicated than chess. I'd like to see you try to figure it out."

Lewis had muttered something and had clammed up.

But Tammy Townsend was still talking. "You'd never in the world catch me making a fool of myself like that. And in front of all those people."

Ellen saw Tammy's flute balanced across the thick bulge of her thighs. No, never in the world would you ever catch Tammy making a fool of herself like that. Nobody would ever ask her to.

She looked down at the song girls. They were the chosen ones. The ones with the shining hair and the shining smiles. The ones the football players noticed, kidded, dated, took to the after-game dances.

Well, Ellen thought. I'm going to the dance tonight too. She turned and waved to George in the trumpet section, two rows behind.

Muir had lost the toss. The offensive team stood along the sidelines, their backs to the stands. Even if that big 60 hadn't been on Leo's jersey, Ellen knew she'd have had no trouble picking him out. Those identical red and gold game shirts, those gold pants stretched over knee pads and hip pads and heaven knows what other mysterious pads couldn't disguise him.

"Aren't you going to play, for Pete's sake? Honestly!"

Mr. Davis, the band director, had his baton raised, and the band swung into "California Dreaming."

Ellen couldn't find the music. She rifled quickly through her stack, taking pages from the clip.

Tammy's eyes rolled in another silent "Honestly!"

And it was then that disaster struck.

A fluky gust of the Santa Ana wind whirled over the stands, lifted all of Ellen's music, and scattered it in a flurry of white squares.

"Oh, no." She grabbed hopelessly at a couple of sheets that were within reach. Some of them already fluttered along the sidelines. What if they blew on the field? What if Muir got penalized for delay of game and it was her fault?

She shoved her flute into Tammy's hands.

"Honestly!" Tammy said.

Ellen rushed down to the sidelines where some little kids were already scooping up the sheets. She crouched behind the line of players.

They shuffled and scuffed their feet in the dry dirt. One giant-sized football shoe mashed a music sheet and ground it relentlessly.

Ellen touched the red and yellow striped sock with a timid hand. "Excuse me. Could you move your foot?"

The black shoe lifted, a head turned down in her direction, and — oh my gosh! Leo the Lion.

"What the heck are you doing?" His voice was anything but friendly.

Ellen scrambled up. Bits of grass clung to the knees of her baggy red pants.

"S . . . sorry," she muttered. "I . . . my music." She pushed her hair back with the hand that held the crumpled sheets.

Leo's golden eyes were narrowed. Suddenly they opened wide, and he smiled. "Oh," he said, "it's you. You're Ellen, aren't you?"

Ellen's heart did a flip-flop into her throat. "Ellen?" She sounded as if she'd never heard her name before. Dumb, dumb. She coughed. "Ellen. Yes."

"Are you coming to the dance tonight?" The words were caught in another gust of wind and whirled away. Surely she couldn't have heard right?

She nodded.

"Good," Leo said.

"Carlton!" The coach's voice swung him back around to the field.

Ellen stood behind him. She could still hear her heart, but now it was thumping like one of the timers Mr. Davis used to get the music beat right.

"**H**ere." A little kid jammed some dirty music sheets into her hands.

"I think that's all of them," George said. And there he was, too, smiling that nice lopsided smile, holding out more of her dumb music.

"Thanks, George," Ellen said.

She climbed like a sleepwalker back to her seat in the stands.

Tammy sniffed, "Honestly! If I'd been you, I would have died."

"I almost did," Ellen said. With nerveless hands she began to rearrange her music.

What was it he'd said? "Are you coming to the dance?" And then he'd said, "Good." What did that mean? What in the world did it mean? And he'd known her name.

"First and ten, do it again. We like it, we like it," the cheerleaders sang joyously. Offense in! Leo in!

Did he mean he'd see her at the dance? Dance with her? But how could he when she'd be there with George? Maybe he thought she was going along with a bunch of girls. Some of the kids did that. But she'd never had the nerve. She remembered the way the golden curls escaped from the sides of the helmet. He had a little mole just at the side of his mouth. She hadn't noticed that before. Of course, she'd never been that close to him before. And it didn't show in any of his pictures.

"We've got the ball, so let's go, let's go. We've got the ball, so . . . let's go."

She seemed to be hearing everything through a haze, through a blur.

What if she told George she couldn't go after all. What if she went alone? The thought came so quickly that it stunned her. Now that was rotten all right. That was really rotten. She'd never, never . . .

"Uh-oh," Tammy Townsend said. She popped a piece of gum into her mouth and sat forward expectantly. "Someone is hurt."

"Injured player on the field," the announcer called.

Ellen raised her head.

A crumpled heap of red and yellow lay very still on the grey-green grass. No need to check the numbers of the other guys standing around. She knew who it was. There wouldn't be this terrible, empty sense of despair for anyone else.

Down below, the song girls danced in a circle, tossing their heads and laughing.

"Beat 'em, bust 'em, that's our custom. Beat 'em, bust 'em, that's our custom."

Injured player on the field, Ellen wanted to shout. Were they deaf or something? They didn't care. Neither did the peanut seller who had stopped at the end of the opposite row to shout, "Get your peanuts, one quarter!"

How could they be so callous? How could they?

"Shut up," Ellen yelled at him. "Nobody wants your peanuts. We've got an injured player out there."

Dr. Ramadan and the varsity coach were running out onto the field.

The red and gold figure stirred, tried to sit, fell back.

"Oh, please," Ellen whispered.

Now they were half carrying him off the

field. He hung upright between them, and his left leg trailed limply behind him.

At the edge of the field they laid him on a bench, unlaced his shoe, and peeled off the red and yellow sock. Leo lay on his back, one arm across his eyes.

The song girls clustered around him. Ellen saw Vicki squeeze his arm.

Dr. Ramadan was probing the knee, and Leo was squirming on the bench, writhing away from his touch.

Ellen heard herself whimper. She wanted to look away, but she couldn't.

The song girls were making pretty, helpless gestures at the crowd.

Now the game was starting again.

Someone else was in Leo's place. A Muir player must have done something good because there was a roar from the crowd, and the coach left Leo and ran to the sidelines.

Ellen wanted to cry. Didn't anybody care?

The ambulance that waited through all the games crept silently along the track.

The doctor helped Leo to stand on one leg.

"Aren't we going to play something?" Ellen whispered. "Injured player, you guys. Don't we at least play the fight song for an injured player?"

"No, we don't," Tammy said. "How dumb. Honestly!" She went back to picking lint off her uniform jacket.

The ambulance had stopped.

Without another thought Ellen stood up.

The high, clear notes of the flute rose sweet and true over the heads of the band. The fight song! And then she heard what she was playing, heard the melody, the melody that to her was always Leo. She tried to slide out of it and into the other song, but her stiff fingers didn't belong to her. This was the only tune she knew, had learned, could remember.

*Nobody knows how I feel about you,
Nobody knows but me....*

Tammy was staring up at her as if she'd gone mad.

Her fingers faltered. Now everybody knew. Everybody!

But someone else had joined in. No, someone else was playing the Monarch fight song, playing it loudly. The trumpet drowned out the flute.

Now some others had added their sounds. She heard more trumpets and a tuba and the loud boom of the bass drum all playing together as the medics lifted Leo and eased him into the back of the ambulance.

She watched till the red taillights disappeared. It was minutes before she remembered about George and what he'd done. How did you thank someone for helping you out on a thing like that? For helping you cover up the way you felt about another boy?

Tammy had slid a little away from her, as if she'd suddenly become contagious.

Ellen turned around.

George was looking right at her and smiling his lopsided smile. But it wasn't the same smile. There was hurt in it, and something else. Disappointment maybe.

"Thank you," Ellen mouthed. It was all there was to say, and it would have to do.

After their halftime show, she went over to where George was standing in line at the snack stand.

The halftime show had been terrible, a torture. Playing, marching, counting steps and beats when she wanted to think about Leo. But now it was over.

The line ahead of George was shorter than the line behind him. "You want me to get you a Coke?" he asked. His glance touched her once and slid away.

"No, thanks," Ellen said. She clasped her hands behind her back. Should she let the whole thing go? Or should she try to explain? Maybe George hadn't figured out why she'd been playing "Nobody Knows."

George moved a few steps with the line. "It's OK, you know," he said. "Nobody knows but me."

Those words!

"You don't understand . . . ," Ellen began.

"Oh, I understand. I wasn't directly behind you. I could see your face."

"Oh." Ellen twined her fingers desperately, one on top of the other.

"One thing, though," George added. "Do you still want to go to the football dance tonight?" His dark eyes watched her closely, and Ellen remembered how she'd asked herself just why she wanted to go so badly. She felt warmth creep up her neck and over her face.

"I see," George said. "Well, I think I want to call it off myself anyway." The line moved again, and he went with it.

Ellen stood very still. She had to wet her lips before the words would come out. "OK. Let's just forget it."

The hurting inside her was almost more than she could bear. She didn't know if it was for Leo or for George or for herself. She carried it with her all night, like a rock in her pocket that she couldn't throw away.

"I thought you were going to the football dance, hon," her mom said later as she lay on the couch, watching TV.

"I was," Ellen said. "But I don't feel well." It was the truth. She felt terrible.

Even her flute couldn't ease the hurt.

In the quiet night hours she played it, looking for comfort. But there was none. When the idea did come, it seemed so simple and so right. She'd go to see Leo. It was a hospital, wasn't it? And he did know her, knew her name, had all but invited her to the dance.

She called the hospital first thing in the morning. "Visiting hours are two till four," a woman's voice informed her.

"Two till four." She repeated the words like a charm. Was that when the world changed?

Was that when the magic started?

After lunch she got dressed in her new Huggy jeans and her embroidered Mexican shirt. She dabbed on perfume and put a little mascara on her eyelashes. Vicki Smith wore a ton of mascara, which probably meant that Leo liked it. But she wasn't Vicki. She wasn't even close. But he'd said, "You're Ellen." He had known her.

She held on to the memory of his voice saying her name as the bus neared the hospital. The streets were Sunday quiet. Palm fronds, downed by last night's winds, lay scattered in ragged brown piles. Kids rode skateboards. A couple of times she felt like giving up and climbing off the bus to safety. But the thought of Leo kept her in her seat.

She bought three big red apples in a little corner market across from the hospital. The market had single roses for sale too, all wrapped in gold foil, ready for giving. What if she bought Leo one of those? What if he said, "Ellen, I've wanted to give you a red rose since the first day I noticed you in algebra"?

"When was that, Leo?" She'd be peeling the foil off the rose, placing it in a slender vase . . .

"Will that be all, Missy?" The market man was smiling a gold-toothed smile.

"Yes . . . yes, that's all." She paid for the apples and walked out into the sunshine.

"Third floor," the hospital receptionist said without even looking up. "Room three forty-three."

Ellen stood in a corner of the elevator. Second floor. Still time to hop off. She couldn't understand where her splendid middle-of-the-night courage had gone. Her sweaty hands made gross black marks on the brown paper sack.

Third floor. Her feet moved her out and along the corridor.

All was quiet inside room 343. Maybe he was asleep, his gold hair curling across the pillow. She lifted a shaking hand to knock on the door when suddenly the quiet of the room inside exploded with laughter.

Ellen stepped back quickly. He had visitors, lots and lots of visitors, it sounded like. No way would she go in. She felt almost a relief in having an excuse to turn back.

Then abruptly the door of 343 jerked open. One of the Muir song girls stood half in and half out of the room. "Hi," she said. "You here to see Leo? I'm just leaving. But I had to hear the end of the joke." She stood aside. "It was a rotten joke anyway. You're lucky you missed it."

Beyond her Ellen saw the small hospital

room. It was jammed with kids. "I don't think . . . ," she began.

"Who is it, Gigi?" That was Leo's voice, as chipper as could be.

"Someone for you." Gigi didn't say her name. Gigi probably didn't know her name. All the heads inside were turned toward the door. There was nothing to do but go in.

It seemed to take as long to walk to the bed as it would have to walk across the Sahara.

Every single inch of space seemed to be filled with bodies, and every single ounce of air seemed to have been used up and used over again. Ellen felt herself gasping like a toad in the sun. And there was Leo, unfamiliar Leo in a white hospital gown with a round, tight neck band.

"Hi," Ellen said. She saw Vicki sitting cross-legged at Leo's feet. She held out the sweaty apple bag. "I brought you these."

"Gee, thanks." Leo took the sack and peered into it. Ellen plucked at the corner of a sheet, letting her hair fall across her hot face. Why, oh why, oh why . . . ?

She looked up in time to catch Leo's desperate glance at Vicki, in time to see him spread his hands in an "I don't know who she is" gesture. He didn't know. He didn't know her.

"I'm Ellen," she said weakly. "From the band."

Leo's face changed. "Sure. When George pointed you out, you were in that creepy band uniform. I guess I've never seen you without it."

George! What was he talking about?

"Give Ellen your seat, Thompson, you big oaf," Leo ordered. A huge guy moved and waved Ellen to his chair.

"George isn't here yet," Leo added.

"George who?" Vicki asked.

"You know George, my algebra tutor."

"Oh, the goony genius," someone said.

A fake high voice mocked, "One of the boys in the band, how sweet."

Ellen looked at Leo. He was laughing. They were all laughing, and it bugged her because somehow it was against George. "You mean George tutors you in algebra?" she asked.

"Sure." Leo's eyes were suddenly wary. "I bet he's told you what a dummy I am."

Ellen shook her head. "No," she said slowly. "George just said that anybody who plays football has to have brains."

"Right on, George," Thompson said. "He's not such a goon after all."

Everything was clear to Ellen now, super clear. She imagined George pointing her out to Leo, saying they might be going to the dance. Leo looking, wondering what George saw in her.

"And George is coming here now? To talk to you about algebra?" Vicki asked. "What a drag!"

"It's probably a drag for George, too," Ellen said. Where did this bunch get off making fun of George? It was incredible how defensive she felt.

Vicki stood up with a flash of long, honey golden legs. "Yeah. Well, I don't need any algebra lesson. Anybody coming?"

The room was full of moving bodies. Ellen stood too.

"But you're waiting for George, aren't you?" Leo asked.

Ellen sat again on the edge of her chair.

Sure she was. What other excuse did she have for being there? George was saving her again, even if he didn't know it.

It was quiet when everyone had gone.

"Does your knee hurt?" Ellen asked.

"Yeah. But they took X rays. It's not too serious. I'll be out in a couple of days."

"Oh." Ellen stared at her sandals. She couldn't think of another thing to say. What had she talked about to George? Everything. Books and movies and hamsters and music and the band. There was a book on Leo's table, *Watership Down*. What a relief! She nodded toward it. "It's terrific, isn't it?"

Leo shrugged. "I haven't started it yet. I'm not much into reading."

"Oh," Ellen said again. She wished George would hurry up and come. And what kind of craziness was that? Here she was, alone with Leo Carlton!

"So, how's the algebra coming?" she asked.

Leo frowned. "It's a pain. But coach wants to make sure I pass it. It could be worse. George is interested in football and the different plays and stuff. I guess it's the closest a guy like George . . ." He stopped, as if he realized he was talking to a friend of George.

"George is interested in a lot of things," Ellen said slowly. She looked closely at Leo. "Don't you like him?"

"Sure. He's OK." The lion eyes slid away from hers.

"But if you like him, why didn't you stick up for him when . . ." Ellen stopped.

The silence stretched between them. It wasn't a good silence, the kind that lies warm and comfortable between friends.

Leo polished one of the apples on the sheet. He was gorgeous, there was no doubt about it. He was all tanned and gilded and glowing. He was just the same, wasn't he?

He took a bite out of the apple. His nose wrinkled, and he abandoned the rest of the apple on the bedside table.

Ellen saw it there, the inside all mushy yellow under the shiny, red skin. Not bad exactly. Just not up to expectations.

That's the way it goes sometimes, Ellen thought. She smiled and stood up.

"I think I'll wait for George outside," she said. George would understand. Funny how sure she was about that.

"Well, OK." Leo sounded relieved. About as relieved as she was to go.

"Good-bye," Ellen said.

It had been a good dream that she'd had for a long time, so she closed the door gently on it. Then she ran down the stairs and out into the sunshine . . . to wait for George.